Dark Side of the Spoon

The Rock Cookbook

LAURENCE KING

Published in 2017 by
Laurence King Publishing Ltd
361–373 City Road
London EC1V 1LR
e-mail: enquiries@laurenceking.com
www.laurenceking.com

Editors: Joseph Inniss, Ralph Miller and Peter Stadden
Text: Joseph Inniss and Ralph Miller
Graphic design: Peter Stadden

Cover illustration by Tom Bunker
© illustrations 2017 (see illustrators listed on pages 78 and 88–93)
Page 4 illustration © Tom Bunker
Page 37: Tommy Lee, 1985 (Neil Zlozower/Atlasicons.com)

A catalogue record for this book is available from the British Library.
ISBN 978-1-78627-088-7

Printed in China

Dark Side of the Spoon
The Rock Cookbook

INNISS, MILLER & STADDEN

Intro

Great recipes are a lot like the best rock bands. They've got to be crowd-pleasing, with a touch of bravado, and can be enhanced with a flash of improvisation. Every ingredient in a recipe has its own important part to play to deliver a truly memorable performance. Whether you're cooking up a mean solo or jamming in a group, *Dark Side of the Spoon: The Rock Cookbook* will cater for all tastes.

Rock 'n' roll is littered with culinary links, from Guns N' Roses' *Appetite for Destruction*, to System of a Down's *Chop Suey* and Ozzy Osbourne biting the head off a bat (rest assured, there are no bat recipes here). This book aims to further bridge the gap between food and rock.

This is our second pun-tastic recipe book following on from *Rapper's Delight: The Hip Hop Cookbook*. This time round, we are celebrating the best of rock with easy-to-cook dishes. Each recipe is inspired by rock legends past and present and is accompanied by an illustration created exclusively for the book by our favourite artists.

Dark Side of the Spoon contains 30 delicious recipes devised for cooks of all abilities. Some dishes are like a catchy riff – simple, but effective; while others are like listening to an epic LP – complex, longer-lasting, but hugely rewarding.

We've designed this book to be as accessible as possible and nothing should be too tricky for any cook with an open mind. The volume dial on each spread shows how much culinary skill will be required to serve up your festival of flavours (like Spinal Tap's amp, this goes up to 11). The B.P.M. (or Beats Per Minute) scale indicates how long each recipe takes to prepare and cook.

All recipes serve four people, but can easily be scaled down or up by increasing or decreasing the ingredients, so it won't matter how many groupies you're catering for.

The Equipment Matrix on pages 8–9 tells you exactly what you'll need before you start cooking. The Supporting Acts section includes our favourite accompaniments to help turn your meal into a feast. There's also an Advanced Methods section (pages 84–87), for those of you who are more confident in the kitchen or want to try something a little more ambitious.

We hope this book will entertain and elevate you to rock-god status in the kitchen. Bon appetit!

The Dark Side of the Spoon team
darksideofthespooncookbook.com

Contents

Contents

Contents

Equipment Matrix

This is a list of equipment that you might need to cook the dishes in this book. For most recipes we assume you have standard kitchen equipment such as saucepans, frying pans, mixing bowls, a colander and an oven, but this matrix is designed to highlight more unusual things you might need for specific recipes.

Preparation

Fleetwood Mac & Cheese
Pig Floyd
Tofu Fighters
Beef Patty Smith
Captain Beeftart
Suzi Quatro Formaggi
Slip Gnocchi
Status Pho
The Offspring Rolls
Dim Sum 41
Tex-Mex Pistols
Mötley Stüe
ZZ Top
Metallikatsu Curry
Ramenstein
Smoked Haddock on the Water
Ladle of Filth
Primal Bream
Def Sheppard
Limp Brisket
Iron Raisin
Slayer Cake
The Rolling Scones
Smashing Pumpkin Pie
Nirvana Split
Spinal Tapioca
Dire Dates
Sepultempura Fried Ice Cream
Judas Peach
Whitesnaked Alaska

Preparation

Equipment	Wok	Tongs (heatproof)	Steamer	Sieve	Rolling pin	Pastry cutter (circular 5cm/2inch)	Pastry/glazing brush	Ovenproof baking dish	Muffin tin	Large mixing bowl	Large bowl (mixing bowl fits into)	Large saucepan with lid	Large saucepan	Large saucepan (inner)	Ladle	Kitchen paper	Electric whisk/hand whisk	Freezable bowl (up to 10cm/4inch)	Deep-fat fryer	Deep, large frying pan	Cooling rack	Cling film	Casserole dish with lid	Tart tin (round 23cm/9inch)	Cake tin (round 23cm/9inch)	Blow torch	Blender/food processor	Baking tray with rack	Baking paper/parchment	Baking beans
								•			2																			
					•					•																		•		
				•																										•
						•				•																				
						•	•			•									•							•		•		
						•	• •			•																		•		
						• •				•					•															
										•							•													
	• •				•				2						•					•							•		
			•			•				•			•						•						•			•		
		•								•												•								
					•					•																				
						•					2	•																		
					•					2	•																		•	
									•				2	•	•															
				•																					•					
						•																				•				
					2					•																				
						•			•															•						
		•				2 •																		•						
	•					3				•						•			•						•					
	•					•										•								• •						
•	•					•	2					•						•												
		•					•																							
	•					•										•			•											
	•					2	•												•											
				•					•			•																	•	
		•					•																							
			•												• •			•												

9

fleetwood mac & Cheese

You Can Cook Your Own Way (... but we suggest this way)

Starters

Difficulty

Description

Crispy cauliflower macaroni and cheese.

B.P.M.

25 minutes preparation
25 minutes cooking

Ingredients

1 cauliflower
400g / 14oz macaroni
A drop of olive oil
60g / 2oz butter
4 tablespoons plain flour
350ml / 12fl oz whole milk
200g / 7oz extra mature
Cheddar cheese, grated
1 teaspoon Dijon mustard
Salt and freshly ground
black pepper

Method

1. Trim the leaves and stalk from the cauliflower and cut the head into quarters.
2. Put the cauliflower quarters in a large saucepan of boiling water with the macaroni. Add a pinch of salt and the olive oil to prevent the macaroni pieces sticking together. Cook for 20 minutes until the cauliflower breaks up.
3. While the pasta and cauliflower are cooking pre-heat the oven to 200°C / 400°F / Gas Mark 6 and make the cheese sauce.
4. Melt the butter in a saucepan over a medium heat, then add 2 tablespoons of the flour and whisk.
5. Add the rest of the flour half a tablespoon at a time to ensure there are no lumps. When you have made a rough paste, gradually add the milk, whisking continuously to make the mixture as smooth as possible. Cook the sauce, stirring, for 3–4 minutes until it has thickened.
6. Add 125g / 4½oz of the Cheddar cheese and whisk until smooth. Add the mustard and stir until thoroughly combined.
7. Drain the cauliflower and pasta through a colander and break up the cauliflower (it should break up even more, into smaller pieces).
8. Place the macaroni and cauliflower mixture in an ovenproof baking dish and pour the Cheddar cheese sauce over it, then add a pinch of salt and black pepper and mix together.
9. Sprinkle over the remaining Cheddar cheese.
10. Place in the oven and bake for 25 minutes until the top is crisp and golden. If you want it extra crispy, you can turn on the grill setting at the end for a few minutes.

Pig Floyd

Comfortably Yum

Difficulty

Description

Homemade spicy pork scratchings, served with wholegrain mustard.

B.P.M.

10 minutes preparation
25 minutes cooking

Ingredients

250g / 9oz pork rind
2 teaspoons fine salt
2 teaspoons ground cumin
1 teaspoon dried chilli flakes
3 tablespoons white
wine vinegar
2–3 teaspoons
wholegrain mustard

Method

1. Pre-heat the oven to its highest setting.
2. Slice or cut the pork rind into thin strips (you may find it easier to cut with scissors), about the width of your thumb and the length of your finger.
3. Lay out the slices of rind on a rack on your baking tray, skin side up.
4. Sprinkle the salt, ground cumin and dried chilli flakes over the rinds.
5. Pour the white wine vinegar into a small bowl and dab the rinds with the white wine vinegar using a pastry brush (be careful not to knock the seasoning off the rinds).
6. Place the baking tray in the oven and cook the rinds for 20 minutes (as they cook and crisp up, the scratchings will curve and bend). After 20 minutes, turn the scratchings over so the skin is at the bottom and the fat is at the top and cook for a further 5 minutes.
7. Remove from the oven and serve on a plate or board with the wholegrain mustard.

Tofu Fighters

Learn To Fry

Starters

Difficulty

Description

Honey and ginger tofu stir-fry.

B.P.M.

5 minutes preparation
20 minutes cooking

Ingredients

200g / 7oz firm tofu
1 teaspoon cornflour
A pinch of salt
3 tablespoons sunflower oil
2 tablespoons runny honey
2 garlic cloves
5cm / 2inch piece of ginger
8 spring onions
2 red chillies
1 yellow pepper
1 lime
1 tablespoon soy sauce
2 tablespoons sesame seeds

Method

1. Cut the tofu cubes into 2.5cm / 1inch cubes, put them in a bowl, add the cornflour and salt and toss to combine.

2. Place some kitchen paper on a plate (this is to absorb the excess oil from the tofu).

3. Heat the sunflower oil in a wok on the highest heat possible for 2 minutes.

4. Add the tofu to the wok and cook, stirring, for about 6 minutes until golden and crisp.

5. Remove the wok from the heat and scoop the tofu out and onto the kitchen paper to drain away excess oil. Leave the rest of the oil in the wok.

6. Tip the tofu into a bowl and drizzle the honey over it.

7. Peel and dice the garlic. Peel the ginger, and slice it into fine strips.

8. Cut away the roots from the spring onions then cut the onions into 4cm / 1½inch batons. Cut the chillies and the bell pepper in half, scrape away the seeds, then cut them into thin strips. Cut the lime in half and set it aside.

9. Place the wok on a medium heat and allow the oil to heat for 30 seconds.

10. Add the garlic, ginger, spring onions, chillies and pepper and cook for 5 minutes, stirring constantly.

11. Squeeze the juice from both halves of the lime into the wok and add the soy sauce.

12. Divide the mix from the wok into bowls, then distribute the tofu between the bowls, placing it on top of the mix. To finish, sprinkle half a tablespoon of sesame seeds over each serving.

Beef Patty Smith

Because The Night Belongs To Burgers

Starters

Difficulty

Description
Burger sliders served with greens and Cheddar cheese.

B.P.M.
15 minutes preparation
15 minutes cooking

Ingredients
4-6 bread rolls
3 garlic cloves
1 red onion
1 tablespoon butter
500g / 18oz beef mince
A pinch of salt
1 teaspoon ground black pepper
1 teaspoon dried chilli flakes
2 teaspoons hot smoked paprika
1½ teaspoons ground coriander
1 egg
100g / 3½oz mature Cheddar cheese
1 tablespoon olive oil
A handful of lettuce leaves

Method

1. Use a pastry cutter to cut your bread rolls into small discs. (If you do not have a pastry cutter, use a small cup as a template and cut around it.) Cut the small discs in half to make 12 thin mini burger buns and set aside.

2. Peel and dice the garlic and red onion.

3. Place the butter in a frying pan on a low heat.

4. Put the garlic and onion in the frying pan with the butter and cook for 4–5 minutes until softened, not browned, then remove from the heat and transfer to a bowl to cool for around 5 minutes.

5. Place the mince in a mixing bowl, add the salt and black pepper, paprika and ground coriander, and a few sprinkles of the dried chilli flakes.

6. Crack the egg into a small bowl and beat it, then add it to the beef mince mix.

7. Add the onion and garlic to the mince.

8. Using your hands, bring the mixture together to form a large ball.

9. Break off small chunks of the mixture, about the size of the palm of your hand. Roll these chunks into balls then flatten them to make patties. This mixture should make around 12 patties (depending on their size). Ensure the patties are tightly squished so they won't fall apart in the pan.

10. Cut the Cheddar cheese into small chunks and set them aside to add to the sliders later. Place the frying pan on the heat and drizzle with the oil.

11. Place the patties in the frying pan and cook them for 5–7 minutes until they brown – turning them so they brown on both sides. Cook them for longer if you prefer beef well done.

12. Once the patties are all cooked, build your sliders: place lettuce on one half of a bun, add the beef patties and chunks of cheese, then top with the other bun half. Repeat with the remaining patties and buns.

Captain Beeftart

Observatory Crust

Starters

Difficulty

Description

Puff pastry beef tart
with hints of chocolate
and cinnamon.

B.P.M.

40 minutes preparation
30 minutes cooking

Ingredients

250g / 9oz salad tomatoes
1 tablespoon olive oil
300g / 10½oz lean
beef mince
2 tablespoons plain flour
160g / 5⅔oz sheet
puff pastry
2 tablespoons
ground cinnamon
20g / ¾oz dark chocolate
1 egg

Method

1. Pre-heat the oven to
220°C / 425°F / Gas Mark 7.
2. Dice half the tomatoes
and set them aside with the
remaining tomatoes (leave
these whole).
3. Place the frying pan on
a high heat and add the
olive oil.
4. Add the beef mince to
the pan and cook it for
10 minutes until browned,
breaking up clumps of meat
with a wooden spoon.
5. Transfer the mince from
the pan to a sieve and leave
to drain over the sink for 10
minutes. This is important as
it prevents the pastry from
going mushy later.
6. Line 2 baking sheets with
baking paper then dust them
with half the flour.
7. Dust a clean work surface
with the rest of the flour and
lay out the puff pastry, then
cut it into quarters. Place
the pastry pieces on the
baking sheets, leaving space
between each piece.
8. Combine the beef mince
and cubed tomato in a mixing

bowl, stirring thoroughly.
9. Leaving a 3cm / 1inch gap
around the edge of each
pastry sheet, top the pastry
sheets with the beef and
tomato mix.
10. Evenly dust the beef with
the ground cinnamon then
grate the dark chocolate
over the beef.
11. Slice the remaining
tomatoes into strips with
a sharp knife, as thinly as
possible, and lay these over
the beef.
12. Crack the egg into a bowl
and beat with a fork, then
brush the exposed pastry
edges with the beaten egg
using a pastry brush.
13. Place the baking sheets
in the centre of the pre-
heated oven and bake
for 20 minutes.
14. Remove the tarts from
the oven and leave them to
cool on a cooling rack for
5 minutes before eating.

Suzi Quatro Formaggi

Devil Grated Drive

Starters

Difficulty

Description

Four mini cheese pizzas.

B.P.M.

1 hour 25 minutes preparation
15 minutes cooking

Ingredients

165g / 5⅘oz strong white
bread flour (plus extra to dust)
1 teaspoon fast-action
dried yeast
½ teaspoon salt
½ teaspoon caster sugar
1 tablespoon olive oil
2 tablespoons milk
1 tablespoon polenta
(for rolling)
2 garlic cloves
60g / 2oz butter
2 sprigs of thyme
125g / 4½oz mozzarella ball
50g / 1¾oz blue cheese
100g / 3½oz mature
Cheddar cheese
50g / 1¾oz Parmesan cheese
Ground black pepper

Method

1. Sift the flour into a mixing bowl and add the yeast to one side of the bowl and the salt and sugar to the other.
2. Make a well in the centre and add the olive oil.
3. Heat the milk in a bowl in the microwave, or a pan on the hob, until lukewarm. Gradually add the milk to the flour.
4. Pour 115ml / 3¾fl oz of warm water into the flour and mix with your hands until the ingredients come together to form a stiff dough.
5. Dust the work surface with a tablespoon of the bread flour and turn out the dough.
6. Knead the dough for 5 minutes then roll it into a ball.
7. Cover the dough with the large bowl and leave it to rise for 1 hour and 15 minutes, or until doubled in size.
8. Once the dough has risen, pre-heat the oven to 220°C / 425°F / Gas Mark 7 and line a baking tray with baking paper.
9. Sprinkle the work surface with the polenta.
10. Place the dough on the surface and punch it to knock out the air. Knead for around 1 minute then shape into a ball.
11. Divide the ball into 4 pieces. Dust your rolling pin with polenta and roll each piece into a flat base, stretch the bases out as thinly as possible then place them on the lined baking tray.
12. Peel and dice the garlic and place it in a bowl with the butter. Melt in the microwave (or saucepan) for 30 seconds.
13. Chop the leaves from the sprigs of thyme and add them to the melted butter.
14. Spread the butter, garlic and thyme mix over the pizza bases with a pastry brush.
15. Slice the mozzarella ball and divide it between the bases.
16. Slice the blue cheese and divide it between the bases.
17. Grate the Cheddar and the Parmesan and sprinkle them over the bases.
18. Bake for around 15 minutes, or until the base turns golden.
19. Remove from the oven, serve on a plate and sprinkle over ground black pepper to taste.

Slip Gnocchi

Don't Spit It Out

Starters

Difficulty

Description

Italian gnocchi *aglio e olio* (garlic and oil) – spicy chilli and garlic pasta-dough dumplings.

B.P.M.

15 minutes preparation
1 hour 10 minutes cooking

Ingredients

500g / 18oz potatoes
2 medium eggs
A pinch of salt
180g / 6⅓oz plain flour (you may need more for dusting)
4½ tablespoons olive oil
5 garlic cloves
2 teaspoons dried chilli flakes
100g / 3½oz Parmesan cheese
Ground black pepper

Method

For the gnocchi:
1. Place the potatoes (skin on) in a saucepan with water and bring to the boil.
2. Once boiling, reduce the heat and simmer for 50 minutes. Pre-heat the oven to 200°C / 400°F / Gas Mark 6.
3. When they are cooked, drain them, place them on a baking tray and cook in the oven for 10 minutes.
5. Remove the potatoes from the oven, halve them and scoop the potato out of the skins.
6. Put the potato in the empty saucepan and mash, then pass the mash through a sieve into a large mixing bowl to ensure a fine potato mash.
7. Crack the eggs into the mixing bowl with the potato and add the salt.
8. Add 150g / 5½oz of the flour and mix to form a dough.
9. Dust a work surface with the remaining flour, tip out the dough and bring it together to form a ball.
10. Roll the dough into a long, thin snake shape, then chop into small, thumb-sized segments. The gnocchi is ready to cook. (If you're not cooking them immediately, dust them with flour to stop them sticking.)
11. Place the gnocchi in a large pan of boiling water, and add half a tablespoon of the olive oil to prevent sticking.
12. Boil for about 3 minutes – when ready, the gnocchi will float to the surface. Drain the gnocchi in a colander.
For the aglio e olio:
1. Peel and dice the garlic.
2. Heat the rest of the oil in a frying pan over a high heat, add the garlic and the chilli flakes and fry for 2–3 minutes.
3. Remove from the heat and add the gnocchi, stirring to ensure the gnocchi is coated in the sauce, then tip them into a serving bowl. Drizzle over the remaining contents of the frying pan.
4. Grate the Parmesan over the dish and season with black pepper to taste.

Status Pho

Rockin' All Over The Bowl

Starters

Difficulty

Description

Traditional Vietnamese beef pho stock with rice noodles.

B.P.M.

15 minutes preparation
4 hours 15 minutes cooking

Ingredients

1 onion
8cm / 3inch piece of ginger
2 litres / 3½ pints pho bone stock* (optional)
450g / 16oz oxtail
Pho spice packet*
400g / 14oz sirloin steak (approx. 2 steaks)
225g / 8oz instant rice noodles
1 lime

Method

For the broth:

1. Peel the onion and cut it into quarters. Peel the ginger and cut it into small chunks.
2. Place a frying pan on a high heat (don't put any oil in the frying pan).
3. Place the onion and ginger chunks in the frying pan and fry for 10 minutes, turning them every minute or so.
4. After 10 minutes, the outside of the onion should be lightly charred (don't worry if the ginger doesn't char). Remove from the heat and transfer the onion and ginger to a saucepan.
5. If you're using your own pho bone stock* add this to the saucepan. Otherwise, add 2 litres / 3½ pints of water to the saucepan and bring to the boil.
6. Reduce the heat to a simmer and add the oxtail and the pho spice.
7. Cover the pan with a lid and leave to simmer on a low heat for 4 hours. Once cooked, follow the next steps to make the pho.

For the pho:

1. Place a large heatproof bowl under a colander and tip in the contents of the saucepan – discard the solids in the colander.
2. Transfer the liquid back into the saucepan and place on a low heat to simmer.
3. Slice the steak into thin strips and set aside.
4. Boil a kettle full of water. Put the rice noodles into a heatproof bowl and cover with boiling water. Leave to stand for 3 minutes.
5. Drain and rinse the rice noodles, then divide between 4 serving bowls. Divide the broth between the 4 bowls, pouring it over the noodles.
6. Divide the steak between the 4 bowls, laying them out on top of the rice noodles. Leave the noodles and steak to stand for 2 minutes. Add a wedge of lime to each bowl before serving.

*See Advanced Methods p84 to make your own pho spice mix and pho bone stock.

The Offspring Rolls

Pretty Fly For A Light Fry

Starters

Difficulty

Description

Vegetarian fried Chinese spring rolls (makes 8).

B.P.M.

20 minutes preparation
5 minutes cooking

Ingredients

2.5cm / 1inch piece of ginger
1 garlic clove
125g / 4½oz napa cabbage
125g / 4½oz carrots
85g / 3oz shiitake mushrooms
A handful of mint leaves
A handful of coriander leaves
5 tablespoons sunflower oil
60g / 2oz instant rice noodles
85g / 3oz beansprouts
1 teaspoon soy sauce
1 tablespoon cornflour
8 spring roll wrappers (of the pastry variety, not rice paper)
Sweet chilli dipping sauce* (optional)

Method

1. Peel and slice the ginger into thin strips. Peel and dice the garlic.

2. Slice the cabbage, carrots (peeled) and mushrooms into thin strips. Chop the herbs.

3. Add 1 tablespoon of the oil to a wok, then place the wok on the highest heat possible for 2 minutes. Add the cabbage, carrots, mushrooms, ginger and garlic and stir-fry for 4 minutes.

4. Remove the wok from the heat and tip the mix into a bowl to cool.

5. Boil a kettle full of water. Put the rice noodles into a heatproof bowl and cover with boiling water. Leave to stand for 3 minutes.

6. Drain the noodles and rinse them. Drain again and return to the bowl.

7. Add the cabbage, carrots, mushrooms, ginger and garlic to the noodles, then add the beansprouts, mint, coriander and soy sauce. Mix together.

8. Mix the cornflour in a bowl with 2 tablespoons of water to make a paste.

9. Place a spring roll wrap on a flat surface, then place an eighth of the filling in the centre, leaving a space of around 5cm / 2inch between the filling and edge of the wrap.

10. Fold over one side of the wrap to cover the filling then dab cornflour paste onto the edges of the wrap. Fold in the ends of the wrap then roll it into a neat, sealed roll (the pastry must be sealed to prevent them breaking apart while frying). Repeat with the rest of the wraps and filling.

11. Wipe clean the wok, add the remaining oil and place on a high heat.

12. When the oil is hot, place the rolls in the wok one at a time (avoid them touching each other) and fry them for 3–4 minutes, turning them with tongs until golden brown.

13. Cool the rolls on a cooling rack, then serve with sweet chilli dipping sauce* (if using).

*See Advanced Methods p85 to make your own sweet chilli dipping sauce.

Dim Sum 41

All Filler No Killer

Starters

Difficulty

Description

Small plates of Chinese prawn dumplings and prawn toast served with a spicy sauce.

B.P.M.

30 minutes preparation
8 minutes cooking

Ingredients

1 red chilli, finely diced
3 tablespoons sesame oil
3 tablespoons soy sauce
A handful of beansprouts
1 teaspoon caster sugar
½ teaspoon salt
1½ tablespoons rice wine
500g / 18oz raw peeled prawns
1 packet of dumpling pastry
3 spring onions
2 garlic cloves
1 medium egg
2 teaspoons cornflour
1 teaspoon hot chilli sauce
4 slices of white bread
4 tablespoons sesame seeds
300ml / 10fl oz sunflower oil

Method

For the dumpling sauce:
1. Halve and deseed the chilli, dice it and fry it in a frying pan with 1 tablespoon of the sesame oil for 1 minute.
2. Tip the chilli into a bowl. Add the soy sauce and mix.
For the dumplings:
1. Finely chop the beansprouts and fry them in a frying pan with 1 tablespoon of the sesame oil for 3 minutes until golden, then remove from the heat and tip into a bowl.
2. Sprinkle the caster sugar and the salt over the beansprouts and stir.
3. Add another tablespoon of sesame oil and all the rice wine.
4. Blend half the prawns in a food processor until smooth, add to the beansprout mix and stir.
5. Take a piece of dumpling pastry, place some prawn mix in the middle, then fold over and seal the parcels with damp fingers. Repeat with the remaining pastry and filling.
6. Pour boiling water into the base of a steamer. Place the dumplings in the steamer and cover. Steam for 5 minutes, then transfer the dumplings to a dry frying pan and fry on a medium heat for a minute to crisp up.
For the prawn toast:
1. Cut the spring onions into chunks and peel the garlic.
2. Put the remaining prawns in a blender and add the spring onions and garlic.
3. Yolk an egg* then pour the white into the blender.
4. Add the cornflour and hot chilli sauce, then blend the mixture to make a thick paste.
5. Cut the bread slices diagonally to create triangles.
6. Spread the prawn paste on the triangles so it covers the bread and sprinkle over the sesame seeds.
7. Heat the sunflower oil in a deep saucepan for 2–3 minutes on a high heat.
8. Drop in the bread and cook until brown, turning it once.
9. Place on kitchen paper to soak up excess oil then serve with the dumplings and sauce.

*See Advanced Methods p85.

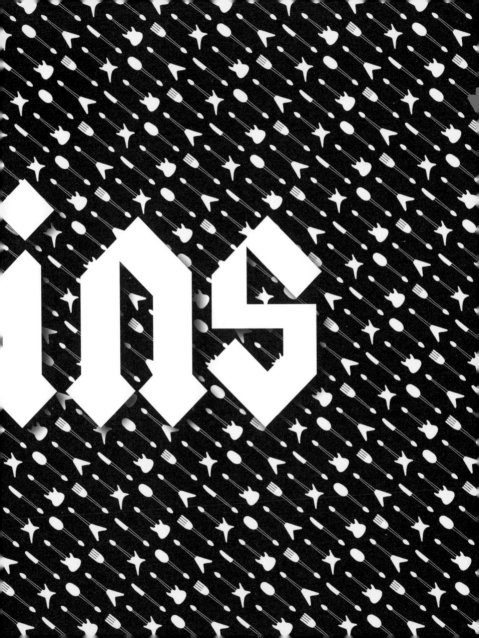

Tex-Mex Pistols

God Save The Bean

Mains

Difficulty

Description

Fajita steak and kidney bean tortilla wraps.

B.P.M.

15 minutes preparation
15 minutes cooking

Ingredients

450g / 16oz skirt steak
Packet of fajita seasoning*
1 red pepper, halved
and deseeded
1 yellow pepper, halved
and deseeded
4 small tortilla wraps
1 tablespoon olive oil
1 red onion, diced
400g / 14oz tinned red
kidney beans, drained
8 large leaves iceberg lettuce
1 tablespoon soured cream

Notes

Any type of frying steak will do, but skirt has the most authentic Tex-Mex flavour.

Method

1. Slice the steak into thin strips (about 10mm / ⅓inch thick) and place in a bowl.
2. Add half the fajita seasoning to the steaks and gently rub the seasoning into the meat with your hands, then set aside.
3. Slice both the peppers into strips (about 5mm / ⅖inch thick).
4. Pre-heat the oven to its lowest heat.
5. Place the tortilla wraps on a baking tray, then place the tray in the oven.
6. Place serving plates on the bottom shelf of the oven.
7. Heat the oil in a frying pan over a high heat.
8. Drain and rinse the kidney beans using a sieve, add to the frying pan with the onion, pepper and remaining fajita seasoning and cook for 5 minutes, stirring continuously.
9. Add the strips of steak to the frying pan and cook for a further 5 minutes, turning them occasionally.
10. Lay a tortilla wrap on each of the pre-heated serving plates. Tear 8 large leaves from the lettuce, then place 2 leaves on each tortilla and add a dollop of the soured cream to each tortilla.
11. Divide the fajita steak strips and beans between each wrap then roll up the wraps and serve.

*See Advanced Methods p86 to make your own spicy fajita seasoning.

Mötley Stüe

with Tommy Leeks

Mains

Difficulty

Description

A warming vegetarian winter stew with 'melt your face off' Gruyère cheese.

B.P.M.

10 minutes preparation
35 minutes cooking

Ingredients

1 leek
3 carrots
5 new potatoes (skin on)
3 tablespoons olive oil
1 pot of vegetable stock (approx. 30g / 1oz)
A sprig of rosemary
A handful of flat-leaf parsley
70g / 2½oz Gruyère cheese
200g / 7oz spinach
Ground black pepper
Sliced bread, to serve (optional)

Method

1. Trim the leek and cut it into thin disks.

2. Peel the carrots and cut them into small chunks and cut the potatoes (skin on) into small chunks.

3. Heat the oil in the saucepan on a medium heat, add the leek and cook for 5–10 minutes. The leek should reduce down and start to brown.

4. Boil a kettle full of water, then mix 600ml / 1 pint of boiling water with the vegetable stock pot in a heatproof measuring jug.

5. Once the leek has started to brown, pour in the stock, then add the potatoes and carrots and simmer for 20 minutes.

6. Strip the leaves off the rosemary sprig and sprinkle them into the saucepan.

7. Tear a few leaves of flat-leaf parsley and sprinkle them into the saucepan.

8. While the stew is bubbling away, grate the Gruyère cheese into a bowl.

9. Place the spinach on top of the stew – it will gradually wilt. Once it has fully wilted, stir it into the stew.

10. Tip the grated cheese into the stew, stir thoroughly and cook for a further 2 minutes.

11. Serve the stew hot, in bowls, and add ground black pepper to taste. Serve with sliced bread, if you like.

ZZ Chop

Sharp Dressed Lamb

Mains

Difficulty

Description

Lamb chops with lime-mint sauce, served with rice.

B.P.M.

30 minutes preparation
40 minutes cooking

Ingredients

3 onions
200g / 7oz carrots
2 tablespoons sunflower oil
8 lamb chops
(approx. 500g / 18oz)
4 large sprigs of thyme
2 limes
1 small jalapeño pepper
1½ tablespoons honey
1½ tablespoons white
wine vinegar
A handful of mint leaves
2 tablespoons olive oil
200g / 7oz basmati rice

Method

For the lamb:
1. Pre-heat the oven to 200°C / 400°F / Gas Mark 6.
2. Peel the onions and cut 2 of them into rough quarters. Peel the carrots and cut them into 5 cm / 2inch batons.
3. Pour the sunflower oil into an ovenproof baking dish and place the lamb chops in the centre. Surround the lamb with the quartered onions, carrots and thyme. Bake in the oven for 40 minutes. While the lamb is cooking, prepare the sauce. Start cooking the rice 15 minutes before the lamb is ready.
For the lime-mint sauce:
1. Cut the 2 limes in half and squeeze the juices of both into a blender.
2. Remove the stalk from the jalapeño pepper. Add the honey, jalapeño pepper, white wine vinegar and mint leaves to the blender and blitz. Pour into a dish and set aside.
For the rice:
1. Boil a kettle full of water (at least 600ml / 1 pint). Dice the third onion.

2. Place a saucepan on a high heat and add the olive oil, then add the onion and stir for 2 minutes.
3. Add the rice to the saucepan and stir to evenly coat the rice in the olive oil.
4. Pour 600ml / 1 pint of boiling water over the rice and onion. Do not stir the rice again. Cover the saucepan with a lid and reduce the heat to a simmer. Allow the rice to cook, covered, for 8 minutes then remove from the heat.
5. To serve, place 2 lamb chops on each plate with the onions and carrots.
6. Divide the rice between the plates and pour the lime-mint sauce over the lamb chops.

Metallikatsu Curry

Master Of Buffets

Mains

Difficulty

Description

Traditional Japanese curry.

B.P.M.

10 minutes preparation
50 minutes cooking

Ingredients

2 onions
1 potato
1 carrot
190g / 6⅔oz jar of katsu curry paste
2 tablespoons olive oil
200g / 7oz basmati rice
1 medium egg
85g / 3oz panko breadcrumbs
4 chicken breasts
5 tablespoons rice flour
10 tablespoons vegetable oil
4 teaspoons fukujinzuke pickled radish, to serve

Method

1. Peel and dice 1 onion. Peel the potato and carrot and cut them into large chunks.
2. Bring 400ml / 14fl oz water to the boil in a saucepan.
3. Add the chopped onion, carrot and potato to the pan. Reduce to a simmer and cook for 20 minutes.
4. Pour in the katsu curry paste and stir. Simmer for a further 10 minutes. While the curry is simmering, prepare the chicken and the rice.
5. Peel and dice the other onion. Heat the olive oil in a second saucepan on a high heat. Add the diced onion and cook for 2 minutes.
6. Add the rice to the second saucepan and stir to coat the rice in the oil. Boil a kettle full of water (approx. 600ml / 1 pint) then add it to the second saucepan. Reduce the heat to a simmer, cover with a lid and do not stir the rice again. Leave to cook for 8 minutes then remove from the heat. Remove the curry sauce from the heat.
7. Crack the egg into a bowl, beat it then set aside.
8. Put the panko breadcrumbs in a bowl and and set aside.
9. Place the chicken breast in a bowl and add 4 tablespoons of the rice flour. Turn the chicken breasts in the bowl so that they are evenly coated in the flour, then pour the beaten egg over the chicken and turn the breasts until well coated.
10. Heat the vegetable oil in a frying pan on a high heat for 2 minutes.
11. Take 1 chicken breast at a time, roll it in the breadcrumbs, then carefully lower it into the oil using tongs. Reduce the heat and cook for 10 minutes, turn it to cook on both sides. Repeat with the remaining breasts.
12. Divide the rice between serving plates. Slice each chicken breast into thick strips, divide the chicken between the plates and pour over the curry sauce.
13. Garnish each plate with 1 teaspoon of the pickled radish.

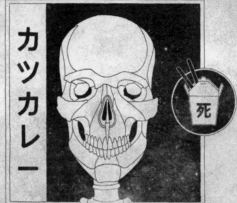
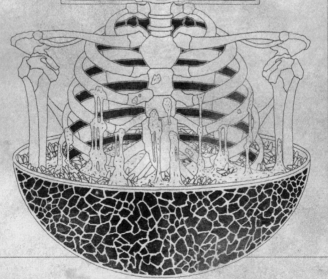

Ramenstein

Du Hast Pork

Difficulty

Description

Japanese pork ramen.

B.P.M.

20 minutes preparation
3 hours 50 minutes cooking

Ingredients

1 large leek
1 carrot
3 onions
9cm / 3½ inch piece of ginger
8 chicken wings
6 garlic cloves
2 tablespoons olive oil
1kg / 35oz pork shoulder
2 green chillies
30g / 1oz shiitake mushrooms
2 teaspoons mixed spice
5 tablespoons soy sauce
2 tablespoons rice wine
6 spring onions
150g / 5½oz bamboo shoots
2 tablespoons rice wine vinegar
4 medium eggs
300g / 10½oz ramen noodles
200g / 7oz spring greens

Method

For the broth:
1. Pre-heat the oven to
200°C / 400°F / Gas Mark 6.
2. Cut the carrot, onions and
leek into chunks. Peel and grate
8cm / 3inch of the ginger.
3. Place the chicken wings,
carrot, leek, onions, whole
garlic cloves and grated
ginger in an ovenproof baking
dish. Drizzle with the oil and
roast for 40 minutes.
4. Once cooked, tip the
contents of the tray into
a large saucepan and add
3 litres / 5¼ pints of water.
5. Cut the fat off the pork
and finely slice the chillies.
Add the pork and pork fat to
the pan with the mushrooms,
mixed spice and chillies.
6. Bring to the boil, then
reduce the heat and simmer
for 2 hours with the lid on.
7. Remove the pork meat and
set aside. Discard the pork
fat. Let the liquid simmer for a
further hour with the lid off.
8. Pass the broth through
a colander set over a large
heatproof bowl - discard the
solids in the colander.

For the seasoning:
1. Peel and grate the rest of
the ginger into a bowl.
2. Add the soy sauce and rice
wine and stir to combine.
Making the ramen:
1. Dice the spring onions
and place them in a bowl.
Add the bamboo shoots and
rice wine vinegar.
2. Warm the broth in a
saucepan on a low heat.
3. Cook the whole eggs in
a separate pan of water for
6 minutes, then peel off the
shell and halve each egg.
4. Cook the ramen noodles
in a saucepan of boiling
water for 2-3 minutes. Shred
the spring greens, add them
to the pan and cook for a
minute, then drain through
a colander.
5. Chop the pork into thin
chunks and place in serving
bowls. Add the spring onion/
bamboo shoots and the
noodles/spring greens.
6. Pour the broth over each
bowl and stir in the seasoning
mixture. Add 2 egg halves to
each serving.

Smoked Haddock on the Water

with Deep Purple Sprouting Broccoli

Mains

Difficulty

Description

Milk-poached smoked
haddock served with steamed
purple sprouting broccoli.

B.P.M.

10 minutes preparation
15 minutes cooking

Ingredients

1 onion
4 garlic cloves
600ml / 1 pint
semi-skimmed milk
200g / 7oz purple sprouting
broccoli
4 smoked haddock fillets
A handful of flat-leaf parsley
30g / 1oz butter
Ground black pepper

Method

1. Peel and dice the onion and garlic.
2. Pour the milk into a deep-sided frying pan and add the
flat-leaf parsley to the milk.
3. Add the diced onion and garlic to the milk and season with
ground black pepper.
4. Place the frying pan on the heat, but be careful not boil the
milk (if it starts to bubble lower the heat).
5. Boil a kettle and fill a separate pan below a steamer and
place on the heat.
6. Add the smoked haddock to the milk in the frying pan and
leave it to simmer for 10 minutes.
7. Place the broccoli in the steamer and let it steam for about
8 minutes.
8. Transfer the fish from the milk to serving plates, then drizzle
over a little of the milk sauce.
9. Add the steamed broccoli to the plate, top with a knob of
butter to melt over it, and serve.

Ladle of Filth
Tortured Bowl Asylum

Mains

Difficulty

Description
Squid ink-drenched seafood and chorizo paella.

B.P.M.
10 minutes preparation
25 minutes cooking

Ingredients
1 red onion
2 garlic cloves
3 tablespoons olive oil
1 pot of fish stock (approx. 30g / 1oz)
2 x 4g / 2 x ⅛oz sachets of squid ink
250g / 9oz Spanish paella rice
150g / 5½oz frozen peas
A ring of chorizo (approx. 225g / 8oz)
200g / 7oz raw shelled prawns
350g / 12oz cleaned squid
A pinch of salt
Ground black pepper

Method
1. Peel and finely slice the onion and garlic.
2. Heat 2 tablespoons of the olive oil in a large saucepan on high heat, add the onion – and cook for 3 minutes.
3. Add the garlic, reduce the heat and cook for a further 2 minutes.
4. While the onion and garlic are cooking, boil 600ml / 1 pint of water in a kettle, then mix in a heatproof measuring jug with the fish stock.
5. Once the stock is mixed in, add the squid ink to the jug and stir thoroughly (the liquid should turn black).
6. Tip the paella rice into the saucepan with the garlic and onion and cook on a low heat, stirring, for 2 minutes.
7. Pour in the inky stock, then turn up the heat so the liquid bubbles. Add the frozen peas to the dish, then turn the heat down to low and cook for around 12 minutes. If the paella looks dry, add more water (2 tablespoons at a time).
8. While the paella rice is simmering, slice the chorizo ring into thin discs. Heat the remaining tablespoon of oil in a frying pan and fry the chorizo for 5 minutes, then set aside.
9. Add the prawns to the same frying pan you cooked the chorizo in and fry them in the chorizo-flavoured oil for 5 minutes until they turn pink, then remove and set aside. Leave the frying pan on the heat.
10. Finally slice the squid (slice the body into rings and keep any tentacles whole), then tip the squid into the frying pan which was used for the chorizo and prawns. The squid will shrivel quickly. Cook for 2 minutes, then tip the squid into the paella.
11. Turn up the heat under the paella saucepan to medium heat, then mix in the prawns and the chorizo and stir thoroughly. Leave to simmer for a further 2 minutes.
12. Use a ladle to divide the paella between bowls and season with the salt and black pepper to taste.

Primal Bream

Breamadelica

Mains

Difficulty

Description

Simple garlic- and lemon-fried sea bream with sweet potato wedges and cherry tomatoes.

B.P.M.

5 minutes preparation
20 minutes cooking

Ingredients

2 sweet potatoes
5 tablespoons olive oil
4 sea bream fillets
(or 2 whole bream, filleted)*
2 lemons
5 garlic cloves
1 teaspoon ground cumin
1 teaspoon smoked hot paprika
12–16 cherry tomatoes
A pinch of salt
Ground black pepper

Method

1. Pre-heat the oven to 200°C / 400°F / Gas Mark 6.
2. Peel the sweet potatoes, cut them into wedges and place the wedges on a baking tray. Toss with 3 tablespoons of the oil and season with the salt and ground black pepper to taste.
3. Place in the centre of the oven and cook for around 20 minutes, turning once using tongs. While the sweet potato is cooking, prepare the bream.
4. Lay the fillets skin side down on a clean plate.
5. Cut the lemons in half and squeeze the juices over your bream fillets – half a lemon per fillet. Set aside the squeezed lemon halves.
6. Peel and dice the garlic and put it in a frying pan with the discarded squeezed lemon halves, then drizzle with the remaining oil.
7. Sprinkle the ground cumin and paprika over the flesh side of the fillets.
8. Cut the cherry tomatoes into quarters and set them

aside on a plate.
9. Place the frying pan containing the oil, garlic and lemon halves on the heat and, once the pan is hot, add the bream fillets skin side down.
10. After 3 minutes, carefully flip the fish over and cook for up to 10 minutes, until the fish begins to lightly brown and is cooked through. Once the fish is cooked remove the fillets from the pan.
11. Remove the sweet potato wedges from the oven and transfer to a plate.
12. Serve the fish on plates with the sweet potato wedges, drizzling the fish with any cooking juices from the frying pan.

*See Advanced Methods p86 for filleting a fish.

Def Sheppard

When Lamb & Mash Collide

Difficulty

Description

Traditional shepherd's pie.

B.P.M.

15 minutes preparation
1 hour 10 minutes cooking

Ingredients

900g / 32oz potatoes
1 red onion
400g / 14oz carrots
1 tablespoon sunflower oil
500g / 18oz lean lamb mince
1 tablespoon tomato purée
1 pot of meat stock (approx. 30g / 1oz)
100g / 3½oz butter
A pinch of salt

Method

1. Fill a large saucepan with 600ml / 1 pint of water. Peel the potatoes, cut them into small chunks and add them to this pan of water. Set aside.

2. Peel and dice the red onion. Peel and cut the carrots into small chunks.

3. Heat the sunflower oil in a second saucepan. Add the carrots and onion and fry for 2 minutes.

4. Add the lamb to the second saucepan and cook for 8 minutes, stirring to break up any lumps of mince.

5. Add the tomato purée and cook for a further 4 minutes.

6. While the lamb is cooking, boil 300ml / 10fl oz of water in a kettle then mix in a measuring jug with the meat stock. Pour this into the saucepan with the lamb and stir thoroughly before reducing the heat. Leave to simmer for 25 minutes.

7. While the mix is simmering, pre-heat the oven to 180°C / 350°F / Gas Mark 4.

8. Place the first saucepan containing the potatoes on a high heat and bring to the boil, then reduce the heat and simmer for 12 minutes.

9. Remove the saucepan from the heat and drain the potatoes through a colander. Add the butter to the empty saucepan and place it back on a low heat, melt the butter in the saucepan then add the potatoes. Add a pinch of salt and mash the potatoes. Remove from the heat and set aside.

10. Place an ovenproof baking dish on a work surface and tip in the cooked lamb mince and vegetables, spreading it evenly across the dish.

11. Spread the mashed potato over the top of the mince. Use a fork to smooth out the potato, leaving textured lines on the surface.

12. Place the dish in the centre of the oven and bake for 30 minutes, or until the top is golden and bubbling, then serve.

Mains

Limp Brisket

Keep Rollin', Rollin', Rollin' (in spices)

Mains

Difficulty

Description

Rolled beef brisket.

B.P.M.

10 minutes preparation
3 hours 40 minutes cooking

Ingredients

2 packets of fajita seasoning
(70g / 2½oz)*
1kg / 35oz beef brisket
(de-boned and wrapped)
2 red onions
1 pot of beef stock (approx.
30g / 1oz)

Notes

Most butchers can de-bone
and roll the brisket for you.

Method

1. Pre-heat the oven to
180 °C / 350°F / Gas Mark 4.
2. Lay the brisket out in a
casserole dish and coat it with
1 packet of fajita seasoning
(35g / 1¼oz), then rub it into
all sides of the meat.
3. Place the casserole dish,
uncovered, in the oven and
bake for 30 minutes. While
the brisket is cooking, empty
the second fajita packet onto
a large plate and set aside.
4. Once the brisket has
cooked, remove the dish from
the oven. Skewer the meat
with 2 forks and roll it in the
second packet of seasoning
(keeping any remaining
spices for later). Return to
the casserole dish and return
to the oven for a further 30
minutes. While the brisket is
cooking, peel the onions and
cut them into quarters.
5. Place a saucepan on a
medium heat and pour in
650ml / 23fl oz pints of water.
Add the stock and onion
quarters. Bring this mix to a
simmer, then reduce the heat
and cover the saucepan.

6. After the brisket has
cooked, remove the casserole
dish from the oven. Skewer
the meat with 2 forks and roll
it in the remaining seasoning.
7. Pour the contents of the
saucepan into the casserole
dish. Add any remaining
seasoning from the plate
and place the meat in the
centre of the dish. Cover the
casserole dish with a lid and
return to the oven.
8. Reduce the oven
temperature to 150°C /
300°F / Gas Mark 2 and
cook for 2 hours 30 minutes.
9. Once the brisket is cooked,
remove the casserole dish
from the oven. Remove the
meat from the dish and place
on a plate. Cover with foil and
leave to rest for 10 minutes.
10. To serve, slice the beef
thinly across the grain. Pour
the juices and onions from
the casserole dish over the
meat as you serve it.

*See Advanced Methods p86
to make your own spicy
fajita seasoning.

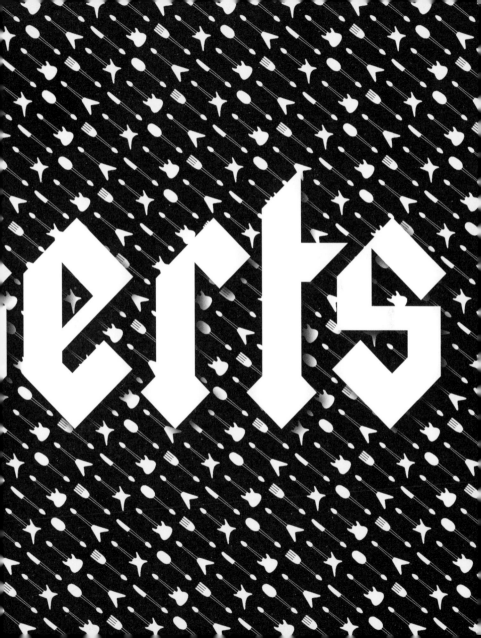

Iron Raisin

Rum To The Hills

Difficulty

Description

Crispy rum and raisin cakes.

B.P.M.

At least 1 hour preparation
(ideally soak the raisins the
night before)
30 minutes cooking

Ingredients

100g / 3½oz raisins
5 tablespoons white rum,
plus extra for drizzling
100g / 3½oz butter
60g / 2oz soft light brown
sugar
1 egg
50g / 1¾oz wholemeal bread
crust (or breadcrumbs)
40g / 1½oz self-raising flour
½ teaspoon ground cinnamon
4 scoops of vanilla ice cream,
to serve (optional)

Method

1. Put the raisins in a mixing bowl, add the rum and leave them
to soak overnight (if you don't have time you can leave them
for an hour, but it is best if the rum has time to be absorbed by
the fruit).
2. Pre-heat the oven to 180°C / 350°F / Gas Mark 4.
3. Grease 4 holes of a muffin tin with 50g / 1¾oz of the butter.
4. In a mixing bowl combine the remaining butter with the
brown sugar.
5. Crack the egg into the bowl and mix well.
6. Put the wholemeal bread crust into a food processor
and blend into breadcrumbs (if you're using pre-made
breadcrumbs you don't need to blend them). Add this to the
bowl and mix thoroughly.
7. Add the self-raising flour and the ground cinnamon.
8. Tip in the rum-soaked raisins and any remaining soaking
liquid. Mix thoroughly.
9. Spoon out the mixture into the greased moulds in the muffin
tin (this mix should make 4 rum and raisin cakes).
10. Place in the oven to bake for 30 minutes (or until they begin
to brown and crisp).
11. Remove the tin from the oven and transfer the cakes from the
muffin tin to a cooling rack. Serve warm with a scoop of vanilla
ice cream and drizzle a teaspoon of rum over each serving.

Slayer Cake

Angel Of Death Cake

Difficulty

Description

A three-tiered angel cake.

B.P.M.

45 minutes preparation
35 minutes cooking

Ingredients

550g / 19½oz unsalted butter
450g / 16oz caster sugar
5 medium eggs
3 teaspoons vanilla extract
450g / 16oz plain flour
2 teaspoons baking powder
300g / 10½oz sour cream
35g / 1¼oz cocoa powder
50g / 1¾oz chocolate chips
300g / 10½oz icing sugar
75g / 3oz dark chocolate, chopped
A jar of strawberry jam
10 raspberries
25–30 blueberries

Method

1. Grease 3 x 23cm / 9 inch cake tins with 50g / 1¾oz of the butter, then line with baking paper.
2. Pre-heat the oven to 190°C / 375°F / Gas Mark 5.
3. Place the caster sugar and 380g / 13½oz of the butter in a bowl and whisk until creamy.
4. Whisk in the eggs one by one until combined, then add 2 teaspoons of vanilla extract.
5. Sift 225g / 8oz of the flour with the baking powder and fold it into the mixture with half of the sour cream.
6. Sift in the rest of the flour (225g / 8oz) and stir in the rest of the sour cream.
7. Divide the mixture between 3 bowls and add ingredients as follows:
Bowl 1 – fold in cocoa powder.
Bowl 2 – mix in chocolate chips.
Bowl 3 – leave as is.
8. Transfer the 3 mixtures into the tins and bake in the oven for 35 minutes.
9. Leave to cool for 5 minutes then transfer the cakes from their tins to a cooling rack.
10. In a bowl mix the remaining 120g / 4oz butter with the icing sugar and remaining vanilla extract.
11. Melt the chocolate in a bowl over a pan of simmering water, then remove from the heat and cool for 2 minutes.
12. Mix the melted chocolate into the icing sugar and butter mixture.
13. Spread jam across the top of the chocolate sponge.
14. Spread chocolate icing on the underside of the chocolate chip sponge.
15. Lift the chocolate chip cake and place it, icing-covered-side down on the jam-covered chocolate layer.
16. Spread jam on top of the chocolate chip sponge.
17. Spread chocolate icing on the underside of the plain sponge, then place it on top of the jam-covered chocolate chip cake so you have 3 layers.
18. Spread the rest of the chocolate icing on the top and sides of the cake, smoothing until fully covered.
19. Decorate with the berries.

The Rolling Scones

If You Try Sometimes, You Get What You Knead

Desserts

Difficulty

Description

Traditional British scones with brown sugar and currants.

B.P.M.

15 minutes preparation
15 minutes cooking

Ingredients

2 tablespoons plain flour, for dusting
60g / 2oz unsalted butter
225g / 8oz self-raising flour
A pinch of salt
60g / 2oz demerara sugar
30g / 1oz seedless sultanas
180ml / 6floz milk
Butter, cream and strawberry jam, to serve

Method

1. Pre-heat the oven to 220°C / 425°F / Gas Mark 7.
2. Line 2 baking trays with baking paper, then dust ½ tablespoon of plain flour over each of the lined trays.
3. Cube the butter and put it in a large mixing bowl with the self-raising flour and salt.
4. Using your fingertips, mix the self-raising flour and salt into the butter.
5. Add 30g / 1oz of the sugar and all the sultanas to the bowl and stir the mix together.
6. Pour 150ml / 5fl oz of the milk into the bowl and stir until the mix forms a soft dough.
7. Dust a clean work surface with the rest of the plain flour. Tip the dough onto the work surface and knead it lightly.
8. Flatten out the kneaded dough and press it down into a sheet that is about 2cm / ¾inch thick.
9. Use a 5cm / 2inch pastry cutter to cut out discs of dough and lay them on the lined and floured baking trays (if you do not have a pastry cutter, use a small cup as a template and cut around it).
10. Collect the off-cuts and lightly knead again, repeating the process until all the dough has been cut into small discs. The mixture makes approx. 10 scones.
11. Using the pastry brush, glaze the tops of the scones with the remaining milk.
12. Sprinkle the remaining 30g / 1oz of demerara sugar over the scones.
13. Place the baking trays with the scones on in the oven and bake for 15 minutes until golden brown.
14. Remove from the oven and transfer the scones to a cooling rack.
15. For best results, serve the scones warm, with butter, cream and jam to taste.

BROWN SUGAR

Smashing Pumpkin Pie

Flava Adore

Difficulty

Description

Classic pumpkin pie.

B.P.M.

20 minutes preparation
(plus cooling)
1 hour 15 minutes cooking

Ingredients

1 tablespoon plain flour
350g / 12oz ready-made
shortcrust pastry*
2 medium eggs
1 x 425g / 15oz can puréed
pumpkin
1 x 400g / 14oz tin
sweetened condensed milk
1 teaspoon ground cinnamon
½ teaspoon ground cloves
1 teaspoon ground ginger
½ teaspoon ground nutmeg
A pinch of salt
Double cream (as much as
you wish)

Method

1. Lightly dust a clean work surface with the flour. Lay out the pastry and roll it until it is around 6mm / ¼ inch thick.
2. Line a 23cm / 9inch tart tin with the pastry and place in the fridge for 10 minutes.
3. Pre-heat your oven to 180°C / 350°F / Gas Mark 4.
4. Take the tart tin out of the fridge and line the pastry with baking paper, then fill the tart case with baking beans.
5. Place the tart tin in the middle shelf of the oven and bake for 15 minutes.
6. Remove the baking beans and baking paper then return the tart tin to the oven and bake for a further 10 minutes.
7. Remove the tart tin from the oven and set aside.
8. Increase the oven temperature to 230°C / 450°F / Gas Mark 8.
9. Crack the eggs into a mixing bowl, then add the puréed pumpkin, condensed milk, ground cinnamon, ground cloves, ground ginger, ground nutmeg and salt. Whisk the ingredients until even in colour and well combined.
10. Pour the mix into the tart case and gently tap the edges of the tart tin to settle the mix.
11. Place the tart in the middle shelf of the oven and bake for 10 minutes.
12. Reduce the oven temperature to 180°C / 350°F / Gas Mark 4 and bake for a further 50 minutes.
13. Take the pie out of the oven and set aside to cool for 10 minutes. Transfer the pie to the fridge and allow to cool for at least a further 15 minutes.
14. While the pie is cooling, pour some double cream into a bowl and whisk vigorously by hand or with an electric whisk until thick.
15. Carefully remove the pumpkin pie from the tin. Serve a slice of pie with a dollop of the whipped cream.

*See Advanced Methods p87 to make shortcrust pastry.

Nirvana Split

Smells Like Teen Spirit

Desserts

Difficulty

Description

Baked peach and banana split with a whisky twist.

B.P.M.

40 minutes preparation
1 hour 10 minutes cooking

Ingredients

4 peaches
3 tablespoons whisky
2 limes
160g / 5⅔oz date nectar
or golden syrup
100g / 3½oz dark chocolate
4 bananas
4 scoops of ice cream
Aerosol (squirty) cream

Notes

For best results, use a whisky aged at least 12 years.

Method

1. Cut the peaches in half and remove the stones.
2. Place the peach halves in an ovenproof baking dish and drizzle over the whisky. Cut the limes in half and squeeze the juice from each half over the peaches. Place in the fridge and leave the peaches to soak for 30 minutes.
3. Pre-heat the oven to 220°C / 425°F / Gas Mark 7.
4. Take the dish out of the fridge and cover the peaches with the date nectar or golden syrup.
5. Place in the oven and cook for 1 hour.
6. While the peaches are baking, blitz the chocolate in the food processor until finely ground (if you don't have a food processor, use a grater or finely chop the chocolate with a knife).
7. Once cooked, remove the peaches from the oven and spoon them into a mixing bowl.
8. Tip the ground chocolate over the peaches and gently turn the mixture, being careful not to break the peaches.
9. Slice the 4 bananas in half lengthways and place each pair of the banana halves in a bowl. Place 2 peach halves on top of each serving.
10. Divide the remaining nectar and chocolate mix between each bowl, pouring it over the banana and peaches.
11. Before serving, add a scoop of ice cream to each bowl and aerosol cream to your taste.

Spinal Tapioca

These Go To Gas Mark 11

Desserts

Difficulty

Description

Creamy tapioca pudding with mini 'Stonehenge' biscuits.

B.P.M.

4 hours preparation
20 minutes cooking

Ingredients

3 medium eggs
700ml / 24fl oz pints whole milk
170g / 6oz tapioca
A pinch of salt
170g / 6oz granulated sugar
4 teaspoons vanilla extract
250g / 9oz butter
140g / 5oz caster sugar
300g / 10½oz plain flour
(plus an extra tablespoon for dusting)

Method

For the tapioca:

1. Break 2 of the eggs into the mixing bowl and beat together, then set aside.
2. Combine the milk, tapioca, salt and granulated sugar in a saucepan.
3. Place the saucepan on a high heat and stir the mixture for 3 minutes.
4. Reduce the heat to low and stir for a further 5 minutes.
5. Remove the saucepan from the heat and continue to stir the mix. Add the beaten egg, a tablespoon at a time, stirring continuously, then stir for a further minute.
6. Place the saucepan back over a medium heat and stir continuously for 90 seconds.
7. Remove the saucepan from the heat for a final time and stir in half the vanilla extract.
8. Divide the mix between 4 serving glasses and leave to cool for 30 minutes, then place in the fridge and chill for 3 hours. While the spinal tapioca is chilling, you can make the 'Stonehenges' as described on the right.

For the 'Stonehenge' biscuits:

1. Turn your oven to Gas Mark 11 (or its highest setting).
2. Combine the butter and caster sugar in a bowl until light and fluffy.
3. Yolk the remaining egg* then add the yolk and the remaining vanilla extract to the bowl. Stir for 1 minute. Add the flour to the mix and stir for 4 minutes.
4. Line a baking tray with baking paper.
6. Dust a work surface with the tablespoon of flour and lay out the biscuit dough.
7. Roll out the dough until it is 5mm / ¼inch thick.
8. Cut it into 12 rectangles about 3.5cm / 1 ⅓inch wide by 10cm / 4inch long and lay them out on the baking tray.
9. Place the tray in the oven and bake for 10 minutes.
10. Transfer the biscuits to a cooling rack to harden.
11. Construct a 'Stonehenge' from 3 biscuits per bowl and serve on top of the tapioca.

*See Advanced Methods p85.

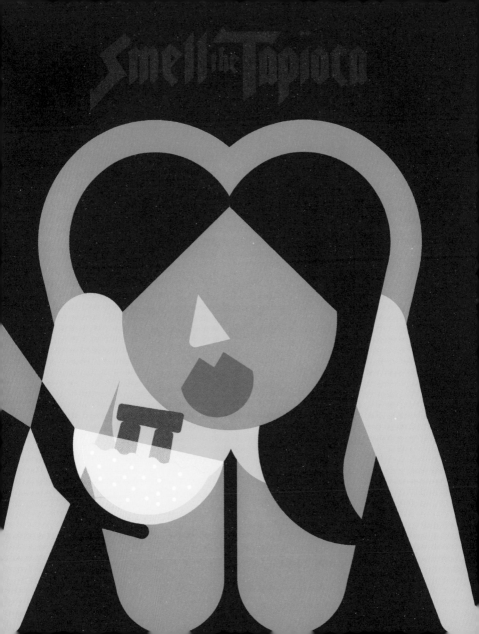

Dire Dates

Sultanas Of Swing

Desserts

Difficulty

Description

Sticky, boozy date and sultana treacle cake.

B.P.M.

20 minutes preparation
45 minutes cooking

Ingredients

200g / 7oz pitted dates
10 tablespoons Cointreau or brandy
270g / 9½oz butter
100g / 3½oz sultanas
270g / 9½oz dark Muscovado sugar
3 tablespoons dark treacle
285g / 10oz plain flour
¾ teaspoon bicarbonate of soda
1 teaspoon baking powder
2 teaspoons ground ginger
A pinch of salt
3 medium eggs
200ml / 7fl oz orange juice
3 oranges
300ml / 10fl oz double cream

Method

For the cake:

1. Roughly chop the dates, then put them in a saucepan and add 7 tablespoons of the Cointreau or brandy.

2. Add the sultanas and warm gently on a low heat for 5 minutes, then set aside.

3. Pre-heat the oven to 180°C / 350°F / Gas Mark 4.

4. Beat 120g / 4oz of the butter in a bowl with 120g / 4oz of the sugar.

5. Add the treacle and beat it into the mix. Beat well for 3–4 minutes until almost fluffy.

6. In a separate mixing bowl, combine the flour and add the bicarbonate of soda, baking powder, ground ginger and salt, and set aside.

7. Crack the eggs and beat them into the treacle mix, one-by-one, sifting in about ⅛ of the flour mix as you go, and stir thoroughly. Once all the eggs are mixed in, sift in the rest of the flour mix.

8. Heat the orange juice in the microwave for 30 seconds (or on the hob in a separate saucepan) until lukewarm,

then pour the juice into the cake mixture and stir.

9. Spoon in the alcohol-soaked fruit and mix, then grate the zest of 2 of the oranges into the mixture and stir.

10. Grease the base of an ovenproof baking dish with 50g / 1¾oz of the butter then line the base with baking paper.

11. Spoon in the cake mixture, then place in the oven and cook for 45 minutes. While it is cooking prepare the sauce.

For the sauce:

1. Put the remaining butter and dark Muscovado sugar in a pan and place on a low heat to melt, stirring thoroughly.

2. Whisk in the double cream, then increase the heat until the sauce begins to bubble. While it is cooking, grate in the zest of the remaining orange and stir thoroughly.

3. Once it is well mixed and warm, add the rest of the Cointreau or brandy and stir.

4. Serve by pouring the sauce over the cake.

Sepultempura Fried Ice Cream

Scoops Of Doom

Desserts

Difficulty

Description

Tempura fried ice cream.

B.P.M.

6 hours 10 minutes
preparation (at least)
12 minutes cooking

Ingredients

8 slices of brown bread
3 tablespoons honey
8 scoops of vanilla ice cream
(or flavour of choice)
Ice cubes (approx. 20 cubes)
85g / 3oz plain flour
A pinch of salt
½ teaspoon granulated sugar
200ml / 7fl oz chilled
sparkling water
Sunflower oil (enough to fill
a deep-fat fryer)

Method

1. Slice the crusts off the
bread and lay the slices out
on a clean work surface.
2. Spread a thin layer of
honey over the top of each
slice of bread.
3. Drop a round scoop of ice
cream (roughly 3cm / 1inch
in diameter) in the centre of
the bread.
4. Wrap the bread slices
around the ice cream balls,
cut away any excess bread
and patch any gaps with the
offcuts (it is important that
no ice cream is exposed).
Repeat this until you have 8
ice cream and bread balls.
5. Tightly wrap each ball in
cling film, twisting the ends of
the cling film to form a round
ball. Place the wrapped balls
in the freezer and leave to
freeze for at least 6 hours
(the longer they are frozen
the better).
6. When ready to serve,
heat the deep-fat fryer to
its maximum setting (the oil
should be very hot).
7. Place several pieces of
kitchen paper on a plate,
ready to soak up any excess
oil from the cooked tempura.
8. Unwrap the cling film
around the frozen balls.
9. Half-fill a large bowl with ice
cubes and position a smaller
bowl inside it (so that the
smaller bowl is surrounded
by ice).
10. Add the flour, salt and
sugar to the smaller bowl.
11. Whisk the sparkling water
into the mix for 1 minute (do
not over-whisk as this will
cause the batter to over-
thicken and absorb too
much oil during cooking).
12. Using tongs, dip one
frozen ball into the batter mix
in the smaller bowl, coat it in
the batter, let the excess drip
off then drop it carefully into
the hot oil in the deep-fat
fryer. Fry to 90 seconds, then
transfer to the kitchen paper
to drain excess oil. Repeat
this process until all 8 balls
have been fried.
13. Serve the balls immediately,
before the ice cream has a
chance to melt.

Judas Peach

Ram It Down

Desserts

Difficulty

Description

A classic crispy and oaty peach crumble.

B.P.M.

10 minutes preparation
50 minutes cooking

Ingredients

5 ripe peaches
½ a lemon
3–4 tablespoons demerara sugar
180g / 6½oz plain flour
100g / 3½oz unsalted butter
A pinch of salt
1 tablespoon porridge oats

Method

1. Pre-heat the oven to 190°C / 375°F / Gas Mark 5.
2. Peel the peaches, then cut them into thin wedges and remove the stones.
3. Place the peach wedges in a small ovenproof dish so they cover the base.
4. Grate the zest of the ½ lemon and mix it in a bowl with the juice of the ½ lemon, then add a tablespoon of the demerara sugar and stir thoroughly.
5. Pour the lemon and sugar mix over the peaches.
6. Place the flour, 2 tablespoons of the demerara sugar and all the butter in a food processor with the salt (if you don't have a food processor you can mix them thoroughly in a bowl with your fingertips).
7. Sprinkle the pastry mix over the peaches and press it down with a fork to ensure that the peaches are thoroughly covered.
8. Sprinkle the porridge oats over the crumble (you can also add a further tablespoon of sugar to taste).
9. Bake the crumble in the oven for 50 minutes.
10. Remove from the oven and leave to cool for 5 minutes before serving.

Whitesnaked Alaska

Here I Go Meringue On My Own

Desserts

Difficulty

Description

A true retro classic with ice cream on a bed of sponge cake and Italian meringue.

B.P.M.

6 hours 30 minutes preparation (at least)
15 minutes cooking

Ingredients

Vanilla ice cream (enough to fill your freezable bowl)
3 medium eggs*
180g / 6⅓oz granulated sugar
Syrup sponge cake (enough to make a circular layer the same diameter as your freezable bowl)*

Notes

Make sure the saucepan you heat the sugar in is very clean – any residue in the pan will ruin the sugar syrup.

Method

1. Place a dome-shaped freezable bowl (no wider than 10cm / 4inch) upside down on top of a piece of baking paper. Use this as a guide to create a circular stencil the same diameter as the bowl.
2. Line the freezable bowl with cling film. Pack the cling film-lined bowl with ice cream, pushing the ice cream down. Flatten the top of the ice cream then cover the bowl with another sheet of cling film. Place this in the freezer for at least 6 hours.
3. Yolk the eggs* then pour the whites into a spotlessly clean large bowl. (Discard the yolks.) Whisk the whites until they form soft peaks.
4. Place a saucepan on a medium heat and add the sugar and 100ml / 3½fl oz water. Heat for 3 minutes and stir, until it turns light brown.
5. Set the electric whisk on its lowest setting and continually whisk the eggs while you very slowly pour the hot sugar syrup down the side of the bowl (don't add the syrup too

quickly, as it will scald and deflate the egg whites). This should take 2 minutes.
6. Turn the electric whisk to its highest setting and whisk the mix for 4-6 minutes, until the meringue is thick and glossy.
7. Cut the syrup sponge cake into a 5cm / 2inch-thick layer.
8. Using the baking paper stencil as a guide, cut a disc of the same diameter as the bowl from the syrup sponge and place the disc on a plate.
9. Take the ice cream out of the freezer and remove the top layer of cling film. Place the flat face of the ice cream on top of the cake disc. This will form a dome of ice cream on top of the cake. Remove the bowl and the rest of the cling film.
10. Spread the meringue mix over the ice cream.
11. Just before serving, use the blow torch to quickly brown the outside of the meringue.

*See Advanced Methods p85 to yolk an egg and p87 to make your own syrup sponge cake.

Support

Supporting Acts

Bruce's Spring Greens

Description
A zesty green walnut salad.

B.P.M.
10 minutes preparation/cooking

Ingredients
2 spring green cabbages
1 lemon
1 garlic clove
30g / 1oz walnuts
1 tablespoon butter

Supporting
Primal Bream, Limp Brisket

Method
1. Slice the spring greens into thin strips and discard the ends. Cut the lemon in half and squeeze the juice into a bowl.
2. Dice the garlic and add it to the bowl with the lemon juice.
3. Chop the walnuts, add them to the bowl with the garlic, and mix.
4. Boil a kettle full of water.
5. Place the spring greens in the saucepan on the heat, add the boiled water and cook for 3 minutes.
6. Drain through a colander and set aside.
7. Place a frying pan on the heat. Add the butter, drained spring greens and the lemon, garlic, walnuts and cook for 2–3 minutes.
8. Remove from the heat and serve – pour over any juices.

Bruce's Spring Greens illustration by Alice Moloney
www.alicemoloney.com

Korn on the Cob

Description
Zingy, herby corn on the cob.

B.P.M.
12 minutes preparation/cooking

Ingredients
A sprig of coriander
1 lime
4 corn on the cob
30g / 1oz butter

Supporting
Tex-Mex Pistols, Limp Brisket

Method
1. Finely dice the coriander leaves and put them in a bowl.
2. Cut the lime in half and squeeze the juices of both halves into the bowl.
3. Boil a kettle full of water and pour into a saucepan, then place on the heat, add the sweetcorn and boil for 6 minutes.
4. Remove the saucepan from the heat and drain the sweetcorn through a colander.
5. Put the butter in the saucepan and place on a low heat. Once it melts, add the coriander and lime and stir.
6. Roll the corn in the butter, mint, coriander and lime, then serve it, drizzling it with the contents of the saucepan.

PoToto Roasties

Description
Deliciously crispy
roast potatoes.

B.P.M.
10 minutes preparation
40 minutes cooking

Ingredients
1kg / 35oz potatoes
A pinch of salt
5 tablespoons olive oil
3 tablespoons polenta
2 sprigs of rosemary
Ground black pepper

Supporting
Smoked Haddock on the Water

Method
1. Pre-heat the oven to 200°C / 400°F / Gas Mark 6.
2. Peel and cut the potatoes into chunks (roughly 5cm / 2inch).
3. Boil a kettle full of water and pour the water into a saucepan.
Add the potatoes and salt and boil for 8 minutes.
4. Once boiled, remove the saucepan from the heat, drain the
potatoes through a colander and return them to the saucepan.
5. Add 3 tablespoons of the oil to a baking tray and place in
the oven for 5 minutes to get hot.
6. Sprinkle the polenta over the potatoes in the saucepan. Hold
a lid over the pan and shake it for 20 seconds to roughen the
surface of the potatoes and coat them in the polenta.
7. Remove the baking tray from the oven and place the
potatoes in the hot oil. Pour over the rest of the oil. Sprinkle
over the needles from the rosemary and black pepper to taste.
8. Place the potatoes in the oven and cook for 35 minutes or
until golden brown, turning them several times to ensure all
sides crisp up. Remove from the oven and serve.

Bachman-Turnip Overdrive

Description
Turnip, carrot and sage mash.

B.P.M.
5 minutes preparation
25 minutes cooking

Ingredients
4 small turnips
3 carrots
30g / 1oz butter
1 teaspoon dried sage
A pinch of salt

Supporting
ZZ Chop, Limp Brisket

Method
1. Peel the turnips and carrots and cut them into small chunks.
2. Boil a kettle full of water and pour it into a saucepan. Place
the saucepan on a medium heat, add the turnip and carrot and
cook for 20 minutes.
3. Remove the saucepan from the heat and drain the turnips
and carrots through a colander.
4. Put the butter in the saucepan and place it on a low heat.
5. Add the turnip and carrot and mash with a masher.
6. Sprinkle in the sage and salt and stir thoroughly.
7. Divide evenly between the plates to serve.

Soundgarden Salad

Description

Garden salad with tarragon.

B.P.M.

5 minutes preparation

Ingredients

1 salad tomato
1 red pepper
1 avocado
100g / 3½oz spinach
100g / 3½oz rocket
2 tablespoons olive oil
1 tablespoon balsamic vinegar
1 teaspoon dried tarragon

Supporting

Tex-Mex Pistols, ZZ Chop

Method

1. Slice the tomato in half, then cut each half into quarters.
2. Halve the red pepper, remove the stalk and scrape away the pith and seeds. Cut the pepper into thin slices.
3. Cut the avocado in half and remove the stone. Using a knife, remove the skin, then dice the flesh.
4. Place the spinach and rocket in a mixing bowl. Add the tomato, pepper and avocado. Mix the salad to ensure the ingredients are well distributed throughout the bowl.
5. Pour the oil into a cup, add the balsamic vinegar and the tarragon and stir thoroughly.
6. Drizzle the dressing over the salad and serve.

Andrew W. Kale

Description

Spicy kale with mushrooms.

B.P.M.

5 minutes preparation
8 minutes cooking

Ingredients

1 garlic clove
30g / 1oz mushrooms
100g / 3½oz chopped kale
1 teaspoon olive oil
1 teaspoon hot smoked paprika

Supporting

Primal Bream, Def Sheppard

Method

1. Peel and dice the garlic. Finely chop the mushrooms.
2. Boil a kettle full of water then pour it into the saucepan. Place on a medium heat and add the kale. Boil for 4 minutes.
3. Heat the oil in a frying pan on a high heat and add the mushrooms and garlic. Sprinkle over the paprika.
4. Remove the saucepan from the heat and drain the kale, then add it to the garlic and mushrooms and cook for a further 3 minutes.
5. Spoon the contents of the frying pan onto plates and drizzle over the pan juices.

Supporting Acts

Advanced Methods

Pho Spice Mix

Ingredients

15g / ½oz cinnamon sticks
15g / ½oz whole cloves
15g / ½oz whole star anise
15g / ½oz cardamom pods
15g / ½oz coriander seeds

Featured in

Status Pho

Method

1. Put all the ingredients in a mixing bowl.
2. Mix the ingredients thoroughly.
3. Fill a muslin cloth spice bag with one portion
(75g / 3oz) of the spice mix and pull the drawstring tight.

Notes

This quantity makes 75g / 3oz spice mix, for one pot of pho.
You can make a bigger batch by increasing the ingredients in
proportion to one another. Store in a jar in a cool, dark cupboard
away from sunlight, and the spices will last around 6 months.

Pho Bone Stock

Ingredients

225g / 8oz fresh beef bones

Featured in

Status Pho

Method

1. Pre-heat your oven to 220°C / 425°F / Gas Mark 7.
2. Put the beef bones on a baking tray, place it in the oven and
roast for 1 hour.
3. Transfer the bones to a large saucepan and cover with 2
litres / 3½ pints of water. Bring to the boil, then reduce the heat
to a simmer. Cover the saucepan with a lid and leave to simmer
for 1 hour.
4. Remove the saucepan from the heat and leave the stock to
cool for 30 minutes.
5. If you have a fat strainer, pour in stock and allow the mix to
fully separate before pouring out. (Alternatively, place a clean
cotton tea towel over a colander. Place the colander and tea
towel over a bowl and pour the stock through to catch the fat.)

Sweet Chilli Dipping Sauce

Ingredients

3 garlic cloves
2 red chillies
3 tablespoons white
wine vinegar
100g / 3½oz caster sugar
A pinch of salt
1 tablespoon cornstarch

Featured in

The Offspring Rolls

Method

1. Peel the garlic cloves and remove any stems from the chillies.
2. Put the garlic, chillies, vinegar, sugar, salt and 150ml / 5fl oz water in a blender then blitz until the mix forms a thin purée.
3. Pour the mix into a saucepan and bring to the boil.
4. Reduce the heat and allow the mix to simmer for 4 minutes.
5. Add the cornstarch a little at a time, mixing with a whisk.
6. Remove the saucepan from the heat and leave to cool for at least 30 minutes.
7. The sauce will keep for around 2 weeks. To store, decant it into a clean glass bottle or jar, seal and leave in the fridge.

Yolking an Egg

Ingredients

1 egg

Featured in

Dim Sum 41
Spinal Tapioca
Whitesnaked Alaska

Method

1. Being careful not to break the yolk, crack the egg in half over a cup and tilt it so that the yolk remains in one half of the shell – some white will drop into the cup.
2. With the other half of the shell in your other hand, tilt the egg shell with the yolk in so that most of the white pours into the cup, then allow the yolk to drop into the empty half of the egg shell.
3. Gently tip the yolk into a second cup. This should give you 2 cups, one with the white in and the other with the yolk in.

Extended Play

Spicy Fajita Seasoning

Ingredients

6 teaspoons cornstarch
8 teaspoons hot chilli powder
4 teaspoons salt
4 teaspoons paprika
4 teaspoons soft light brown sugar
2 teaspoons onion powder / onion granules
1 teaspoon garlic powder
2 teaspoons cayenne pepper
1 teaspoon ground cumin

Featured in

Limp Brisket
Tex-Mex Pistols

Method

1. Put all the ingredients in a mixing bowl.
2. Mix the ingredients thoroughly.

Notes

This quantity makes 85g / 3oz of seasoning – it can be scaled up by increasing the ingredients in proportion to one another.

Filleting a Fish

Ingredients

Fish

Featured in

Primal Bream

Method

1. If the fish has been scaled but not yet gutted, slice open the underside of the fish with a sharp knife and remove the fish's guts using a teaspoon.
2. Cut behind the gills and the wing of the fish, then turn it over. Do the same on the other side so the head comes loose. You can now discard the head.
3. Using the spine as your guide, slice just inside the spine from the tail to the top of the fish – open it up and pull the side it away from the bones.
4. If any of the fillet does not come loose from the bones, use the knife to release the fillet from the body.
5. Turn the fish over and repeat – giving you two fillets, and a bony central part of the fish which can be discarded.
6. Use the tweezers to pull any small bones from the fillet, being careful not to break apart the flesh. Rinse the fillets.

Shortcrust Pastry

Ingredients

100g / 3½oz unsalted butter
225g / 8oz plain flour, plus
1 tablespoon to dust
A pinch of salt

Featured in

Smashing Pumpkin Pie

Method

1. Cut the butter into 2cm / ¾ inch cubes and set aside.
2. Sift the flour into a mixing bowl and add the butter.
3. Using your fingertips, rub the butter and flour together until the mix resembles breadcrumbs, with no lumps of butter.
4. Add the salt and 3 tablespoons of cold water. Using a spoon, mix together to form a dough.
5. Dust the work surface with the tablespoon of flour.
6. Gently knead the dough on the floured work surface.
7. Wrap in cling film and chill in the fridge until required.

Syrup Sponge Cake

Ingredients

200g / 7oz unsalted butter
100g / 3½oz caster sugar
2 medium eggs
4 tablespoons golden syrup
200g / 7oz self-raising flour

Featured in

Whitesnaked Alaska

Method

1. Pre-heat the oven to 180°C / 350°F / Gas Mark 4.
2. Line a cake tin with baking paper.
3. Place the butter and sugar in a mixing bowl and mix together using a fork until it becomes soft and fluffy.
4. Beat the eggs into the butter and sugar, one at a time, then add the golden syrup and mix.
5. Add the flour and mix until smooth.
6. Scrape the mix into the cake tin, level it out with a spatula and place in the oven for 40 minutes or until golden brown.
7. Remove from the oven and set aside to cool on a wire rack.

Recipe Index – Starters

The Recipe Index is your guide to all the recipes in the book, allowing you to see at a glance the difficulty and the time it takes to make each recipe. We have also listed dietary and allergen information, as follows:

⊙ Vegetarian
◎ Pescatarian
◉ Gluten-free

EASIEST
Pig Floyd
1/11

HARDEST
The Offspring Rolls
9/11

QUICKEST
The Offspring Rolls
20 mins/5 mins

SLOWEST
Status Pho
15 mins/4 hours 15 mins

12
Fleetwood Mac & Cheese
Difficulty: 4/11
B.P.M.: 25 mins/25 mins
⊙ ◎
by Eve Lloyd Knight
evelloydknight.co.uk

20
Captain Beeftart
Difficulty: 4/11
B.P.M.: 40 mins/30 mins

by Tom J. Newell
tomjnewell.com

22
Suzi Quatro Formaggi
Difficulty: 5/11
B.P.M.: 1 hour 25 mins/15 mins
⊙ ◎
by Lynnie Zulu
lynniezulu.com

24
Slip Gnocchi
Difficulty: 6/11
B.P.M.: 15 mins/1 hour 10 mins
⊙ ◎
by Ewen Farr
unfarr.com

Extended Play

14
Pig Floyd
Difficulty: 1/11
B.P.M.: 10 mins/25 mins
☺

by Will Finlay
wbfinlay.tumblr.com

16
Tofu Fighters
Difficulty: 3/11
B.P.M.: 5 mins/20 mins
☺ ☺

by Anje Jager
anjejager.com

18
Beef Patty Smith
Difficulty: 4/11
B.P.M.: 15 mins/15 mins

by Annemarieke Kloosterhof
annemariekekloosterhof.com

26
Status Pho
Difficulty: 6/11
B.P.M.: 15 mins/4 hours 15 mins
☺

by Joe Sparkes
joe-sparkes.com

28
The Offspring Rolls
Difficulty: 9/11
B.P.M.: 20 mins/5 mins
☺ ☺

by Matt Robinson
matthewrobinson.co.uk

30
Dim Sum 41
Difficulty: 7/11
B.P.M.: 30 mins/8 mins
☺

by Joe Bichard
joebichard.com

Extended Play

Recipe Index – Mains

Extended Play

EASIEST
Smoked Haddock on the Water
2/11

HARDEST
Ramenstein
9/11

QUICKEST
Smoked Haddock on the Water
10 mins/15 mins

SLOWEST
Limp Brisket
10 mins/3 hours 40 mins

34
Tex-Mex Pistols
Difficulty: 6/11
B.P.M.: 15 mins/15 mins

by Adam Cruft
adamcruft.com

42
Ramenstein
Difficulty: 9/11
B.P.M.: 20 mins/3 hours 50 mins

by Jack Hudson
jack-hudson.com

44
Smoked Haddock on the Water
Difficulty: 2/11
B.P.M.: 10 mins/15 mins
℗ ⓔ
by Cassandra Agazzi Brooks
cassandraagazzibrooks.co.uk

46
Ladle of Filth
Difficulty: 6/11
B.P.M.: 10 mins/25 mins

by Louise Zergaeng Pomeroy
louisezpomeroy.com

36
Mötley Stue
Difficulty: 3/11
B.P.M.: 10 mins/35 mins
🎵 😊

by Hattie Stewart
hattiestewart.com

38
ZZ Chop
Difficulty: 5/11
B.P.M.: 30 mins/40 mins
😊

by Yeji Yun
seeouterspace.com

40
Metallikatsu Curry
Difficulty: 8/11
B.P.M.: 10 mins/50 mins

by Bradley Jay
bradleyjay.co.uk

48
Primal Bream
Difficulty: 3/11
B.P.M.: 5 mins/20 mins
🎵

by Paul Hill (Vagabond Tattoo)
iamvagabond.co.uk

50
Def Sheppard
Difficulty: 4/11
B.P.M.: 15 mins/1 hour 10 mins

by Mudrok
samuelmurdoch.co.uk

52
Limp Brisket
Difficulty: 8/11
B.P.M.: 10 mins/3 hours 40 mins

by Paul Layzell
layzellbros.com

Recipe Index – Desserts

EASIEST
The Rolling Scones
2/11

HARDEST
Spinal Tapioca
11/11

QUICKEST
The Rolling Scones
15 mins/15 mins

SLOWEST
Whitesnaked Alaska
6 hours 30 mins/15 mins

Extended Play

56
Iron Raisin
Difficulty: 4/11
B.P.M.: 1 hour/30 mins
☺ ☺
by Andy Baker
andy-baker.com

64
Nirvana Split
Difficulty: 4/11
B.P.M.: 40 mins/1 hour 10 mins
☺ ☺ ☺
by Patch D. Keyes
patchdkeyes.co.uk

66
Spinal Tapioca
Difficulty: 11/11
B.P.M.: 4 hours/20 mins
☺ ☺
by JMWL
jmwl.studio

68
Dire Dates
Difficulty: 6/11
B.P.M.: 20 mins/45 mins
☺ ☺
by Peter Stadden
peterstadden.co.uk

**58
Slayer Cake**
Difficulty: 8/11
B.P.M.: 45 mins/35 mins
☺ ☹
by Sam Taylor
samtaylorillustrator.com

**60
The Rolling Scones**
Difficulty: 2/11
B.P.M.: 15 mins/15 mins
☺ ☹
by Rob Flowers
robflowers.co.uk

**62
Smashing Pumpkin Pie**
Difficulty: 7/11
B.P.M.: 20 mins/1 hour 15 mins
☺ ☹
by Stuart Patience
stuartpatience.co.uk

**70
Sepultempura Fried Ice Cream**
Difficulty: 10/11
B.P.M.: 6 hours 10 mins/12 mins
☺ ☹
by Pete Sharp
petesharpart.com

**72
Judas Peach**
Difficulty: 3/11
B.P.M.: 10 mins/50 mins
☺ ☹
by Kristian Jones
kristian-jones.co.uk

**74
Whitesnaked Alaska**
Difficulty: 10/11
B.P.M.: 6 hours 30 mins/15 mins
☺ ☹
by Daniel Boyle
treatstudios.com

Extended Play

Dietary Information

Gluten-free - does not contain gluten

These dishes can easily be made without gluten. We recommend you check each ingredient though, as it's not unusual for items to unexpectedly have gluten in them. You can make these recipes gluten-free by doing the following:

Tofu Fighters: Swap the soy sauce for gluten-free soy sauce.
Beef Patty Smith: Swap the bread rolls for gluten-free bread rolls.
The Offspring Rolls: Swap the pastry wraps for rice wraps (although you won't be able to fry them), also swap the soy sauce for gluten-free soy sauce.
Mötley Stüe: Check the stock is gluten-free and swap the bread for gluten-free bread.
Ramenstein: Swap the ramen noodles for rice noodles and check the spices are made in a gluten-free environment.
Ladle of Filth: Check the stock is gluten-free.
Primal Bream: Check the spices are made in a gluten-free environment.
Def Sheppard: Check the stock is gluten-free.
Limp Brisket: Make sure the fajita mix and beef stock are gluten-free.
The Rolling Scones: Swap the flour with gluten-free flour.
Spinal Tapioca: The tapioca is gluten-free but the biscuits are not.
Sepultempura Fried Ice Cream: Swap the bread for gluten-free bread, and use gluten-free flour in place of the plain flour. Make sure the ice cream is gluten-free.
Judas Peach: Swap the plain flour for gluten-free flour and check the oats are gluten-free.
Whitesnaked Alaska: Use a gluten-free cake for the base and ensure your ice cream is gluten-free.

Vegan - does not contain any animal product

You can make these recipes vegan by doing the following:

Tofu Fighters: Swap the honey for a vegan fruit nectar.
The Offspring Rolls: Swap the pastry wraps for rice wraps (although you can't fry them).

Extended Play

Setlist

Have a rock festival in your kitchen. In the official *Dark Side of the Spoon* setlist, every one of the 36 dishes is catered for. For the full *Dark Side of the Spoon* experience, scan the QR code below or visit darksideofthespooncookbook.com. Warning: Some lyrics are explicit. Enjoy!

Extended Play

1. Fleetwood Mac – Go Your Own Way
2. Pink Floyd – Comfortably Numb
3. Foo Fighters – Learn To Fly
4. Patti Smith – Because The Night
5. Captain Beefheart – Observatory Crest
6. Suzi Quatro – Devil Gate Drive
7. Slipknot – Spit It Out
8. Status Quo – Rockin' All Over The World
9. The Offspring – Pretty Fly (For A White Guy)
10. Sum 41 – Fat Lip
11. Sex Pistols – God Save The Queen
12. Mötley Crüe – Girls, Girls, Girls
13. ZZ Top – Sharp Dressed Man
14. Metallica – Master Of Puppets
15. Rammstein – Du Hast
16. Deep Purple – Smoke On The Water
17. Cradle of Filth – Tortured Soul Asylum
18. Primal Scream – Come Together
19. Def Leppard – When Love & Hate Collide
20. Limp Bizkit – Rollin' (Air Raid Vehicle)

21. Iron Maiden – Run To The Hills
22. Slayer – Angel Of Death
23. The Rolling Stones – You Can't Always Get What You Want
24. The Smashing Pumpkins – Ava Adore
25. Nirvana – Smells Like Teen Spirit
26. Spinal Tap – Stonehenge
27. Dire Straits – Sultans Of Swing
28. Sepultura – Troops Of Doom
29. Judas Priest – Ram It Down
30. Whitesnake – Here I Go Again

31. Bruce Springsteen – Born To Run
32. Korn – Freak On A Leash
33. Toto – Africa
34. Bachman-Turner Overdrive – You Ain't Seen Nothing Yet
35. Soundgarden – Black Hole Sun
36. Andrew W.K. – Party Hard

Outro

This book wouldn't be possible without the help of a huge number of people. We would like to say a big thank you to the following people for their support and contribution to the making of *Dark Side of the Spoon*:

Sophie Drysdale, Andrew Roff, Kathryn Colwell and the team at Laurence King Publishing Ltd. Björn Almqvist, Andy Baker, Katie Baxter, Joe Bichard, Daniel Boyle, Cassie Agazzi Brooks, Tom Bunker, Alex Campbell, Fran Carson, Ollie Clarke, Adam Cruft, Stewart Davies, Mary-Jay East, Andrew Ellis (and the Ellis family), Lee Faber, Ewen Farr, Will Finlay, Amy Fletcher, Rob Flowers, Rob Gill, Nic Hargreaves, Robert Hastings, Paul Hill, Jack Hudson, Harriet, Rona, Sue, Vicki and Warren Inniss, Anje Jager, Kristian Jones, Chris Kay, Jae Kerridge, Patch D. Keyes, Annemarieke Kloosterhof, Eve Lloyd Knight, Paul Layzell, Gary Lincoln, Joe Luxton, Mandy, Peter and Penny Miller, Alice Moloney, Rebecca Morris, Hadi Mukhtar, Sam Murdoch, Tom Murphy, Tom J. Newell, Laura Nickoll, Stuart Patience, Tom Peacock, Louise Zergaeng Pomeroy, Garret Power, Sam Ritchie, Matt Robinson, Nicolas Robinson, Lily Samengo-Turner, Pete Sharp, Joe Sparkes, Jessica Spencer, Richard and Sharon Stadden, Lucy Stehlik, Hattie Stewart, Sam Taylor, Edward Whittaker, Yeji Yun, Lynnie Zulu.

Dark Side of the Spoon Community

Keep updated with all things *Dark Side of the Spoon*. We'd love to hear from you!

W darksideofthespooncookbook.com

⊙ @dsotscookbook

🐦 @dsotscookbook

f facebook.com/dsotscookbook

If you enjoyed *Dark Side of the Spoon*, you might also want to check out our other cookbook *Rapper's Delight: The Hip Hop Cookbook*. See rappersdelightcookbook.com for more information.